Tucholsky Wagner Zola Scott Sydow Freud Schlegel
Turgenev Wallace Fonatne Twain Walther von der Vogelweide Fouqué Friedrich II. von Preußen
Weber Freiligrath Frey
Fechner Fichte Weiße Rose von Fallersleben Kant Ernst Frommel
Richthofen
Engels Fielding Hölderlin Dumas
Fehrs Faber Flaubert Eichendorff Tacitus
Feuerbach Maximilian I. von Habsburg Fock Eliasberg Zweig Ebner Eschenbach
Ewald Eliot Vergil
Goethe Elisabeth von Österreich London
Mendelssohn Balzac Shakespeare Dostojewski Ganghofer
Trackl Stevenson Lichtenberg Rathenau Doyle Gjellerup
Mommsen Tolstoi Hambruch Droste-Hülshoff
Thoma Lenz Hanrieder
Dach von Arnim Hägele Hauff Humboldt
Karrillon Reuter Verne Rousseau Hagen Hauptmann Gautier
Garschin Defoe Hebbel Baudelaire
Damaschke Descartes
Hegel Kussmaul Herder
Wolfram von Eschenbach Dickens Schopenhauer Rilke George
Bronner Darwin Melville Grimm Jerome Bebel
Campe Horváth Aristoteles Proust
Bismarck Vigny Barlach Voltaire Federer Herodot
Gengenbach Heine
Storm Casanova Tersteegen Grillparzer Georgy
Chamberlain Lessing Langbein Gilm Gryphius
Brentano Lafontaine
Strachwitz Claudius Schiller Kralik Iffland Sokrates
Katharina II. von Rußland Bellamy Schilling
Gerstäcker Raabe Gibbon Tschechow
Löns Hesse Hoffmann Gogol Wilde Vulpius
Luther Heym Hofmannsthal Gleim
Roth Heyse Klopstock Klee Hölty Morgenstern Goedicke
Luxemburg Puschkin Homer Kleist
La Roche Horaz Mörike Musil
Machiavelli Kierkegaard Kraft Kraus
Navarra Aurel Musset Lamprecht Kind Kirchhoff Hugo Moltke
Nestroy Marie de France Laotse Ipsen Liebknecht
Nietzsche Nansen Ringelnatz
Marx Lassalle Gorki Klett Leibniz
von Ossietzky May vom Stein Lawrence Irving
Petalozzi Knigge
Platon Pückler Michelangelo Kafka
Sachs Poe Liebermann Kock
de Sade Praetorius Mistral Zetkin Korolenko

The publishing house tredition has created the series **TREDITION CLASSICS**. It contains classical literature works from over two thousand years. Most of these titles have been out of print and off the bookstore shelves for decades.

The book series is intended to preserve the cultural legacy and to promote the timeless works of classical literature. As a reader of a **TREDITION CLASSICS** book, the reader supports the mission to save many of the amazing works of world literature from oblivion.

The symbol of **TREDITION CLASSICS** is Johannes Gutenberg (1400 – 1468), the inventor of movable type printing.

With the series, tredition intends to make thousands of international literature classics available in printed format again – worldwide.

All books are available at book retailers worldwide in paperback and in hardcover. For more information please visit: www.tredition.com

tredition was established in 2006 by Sandra Latusseck and Soenke Schulz. Based in Hamburg, Germany, tredition offers publishing solutions to authors and publishing houses, combined with worldwide distribution of printed and digital book content. tredition is uniquely positioned to enable authors and publishing houses to create books on their own terms and without conventional manufacturing risks.

For more information please visit: www.tredition.com

The Corporation of London, Its Rights and Privileges

William Ferneley Allen

Imprint

This book is part of the TREDITION CLASSICS series.

Author: William Ferneley Allen
Cover design: toepferschumann, Berlin (Germany)

Publisher: tredition GmbH, Hamburg (Germany)
ISBN: 978-3-8491-6543-7

www.tredition.com
www.tredition.de

Copyright:
The content of this book is sourced from the public domain.

The intention of the TREDITION CLASSICS series is to make world literature in the public domain available in printed format. Literary enthusiasts and organizations worldwide have scanned and digitally edited the original texts. tredition has subsequently formatted and redesigned the content into a modern reading layout. Therefore, we cannot guarantee the exact reproduction of the original format of a particular historic edition. Please also note that no modifications have been made to the spelling, therefore it may differ from the orthography used today.

PREFACE.

Some apology is necessary on the part of one whose acquaintance with civic affairs is of such recent date, for presuming to stand forth as the champion of the fights and privileges of the City of London. No man of common spirit, however, could tamely submit to the insulting charges and coarse insinuations with which the Corporation has long been assailed by malevolent or ignorant individuals. That the civic system is free from spot or blemish, no one in his senses would pretend to assert. But it may honestly and truly be asserted that the Court of Aldermen have both the power and the inclination to amend whatever is defective, and to introduce whatever reforms are desirable, without the irritating and officious interference of the imperial legislature. The system may not be perfect, for it is of human origin; but its administrators are men of upright character, practically conversant with the requirements of trade, and animated by am earnest desire to promote the interests of their fellow-citizens. Why, then, are they not intrusted with the honourable task of gradually improving the machinery of the civic government, and of completing the good work they have long since spontaneously inaugurated? It might, perhaps, have been better had this pamphlet never taken form and substance. A feeble advocate endangers, and oftentimes loses, the best possible cause; but still, out of the fulness of the heart the mouth will speak, and pour forth sentiments and feelings that no longer brook control. This, at least, is the only excuse that can be offered for troubling the public with the opinions of a comparative novice.

7, LEADENHALL STREET, July 26th, 1858.

CONTENTS.

INTRODUCTORY SKETCH.

London under the Romans
Gilds
Burghs
Charter of William the Conqueror
Reflections
Subsequent Charters
City divided into Wards
Civic Hospitality
The Quo Warranto Case
Restoration of the Charter

PART I.

THE CORPORATION AS IT IS.

The Municipal Constitution
The Lord Mayor
The Aldermen
The Court of Common Council
The Citizens
The Livery Companies
The Sheriffs

The Law Courts
Public Charities
Conservancy of the Thames
The Metage Dues

PART II.

THE CIVIC REFORM BILL.

The Commission of Inquiry
The New Wards
Aldermen and Common-Councilmen
City Expenditure
City Receipts
Removal of Restrictions

THE CORPORATION OF LONDON,

&c.

INTRODUCTORY SKETCH.

London under the Romans — Gilds — Burghs — Charter of William the
Conqueror — Reflections — Subsequent Charters — City divided into
Wards — Civic Hospitality — The Quo Warranto Case — Restoration of the
Charter.

The first historical notice of the City of London occurs in that portion of the Annals of Tacitus which treats of the insurrection of Boadicea. At that time it was a place much frequented by merchants, attracted partly by the natural advantages of the site, and partly by the vicinity of the Roman camp at Islington. It is stated that 70,000 persons, of both sexes and of all ages, were massacred by that fierce heroine in London and at St. Albans; but it must not be supposed that the ordinary population of those two towns could have formed so large an aggregate. It is far more probable that numbers of old men, women, and children flocked thither from the neighbourhood, in the hope of escaping from the violence and rapine of the patriot army. Their expectations, however, were disappointed, as the Roman general deemed it more prudent to evacuate an untenable post, than to risk the dominion of the entire island on the event of a battle fought under adverse circumstances. At the same time the slaughter of the inhabitants justifies the inference that they were foreigners rather than natives, some being traders from Gaul, but the majority either Roman colonists or the followers and hangers-on of the stationary camp. Indeed, it may be gathered from the description of Tacitus, that these traders were chiefly commissariat contractors and brokers or money-changers. The Romans do not appear to have evinced a high order of commercial instinct, nor to have looked upon the development of trade as one of the chief objects of government. Their mission was to overrun other nations, and to prevent them from indulging in internecine warfare. To them mankind are therefore indebted for the preservation of whatever civilization was then extant, and for stopping the retrogressive course of the human race. This was particularly observable in their conquest of Greece and the kingdoms of Asia Minor, where incessant quarrels between rival cities and principalities had checked the progress of the arts, sciences, and literature. Content to conquer in battle, and, as the just reward of their superior prowess, to impose tribute and a governor, they seldom interfered with local customs and usages. Perhaps one great secret of their marvellous success was this systematic abstinence from intermeddling with the local administrations. The principle of self-government was never more fully appreciated than by this remarkable people, who, sending forth consuls, vice-consuls, and prefects, yet left to the conquered the management of their own affairs and the guardianship of their own interests. Not even in the most corrupt days of the empire was it attempted to absorb the patronage of every department and province for the benefit of a few, under the pretext of imparting greater vigour to the administration of public affairs by centralization. It was not deemed wise or necessary to constitute central boards for the direction of matters with which not a single member might, possibly, be acquainted. They did not aim at an ideal perfection, but were satisfied with doing what was practicable, and with a large average of general prosperity. To each civitas—corresponding to our phrase of "city and county"—was assigned the regulation of its own domestic policy, by means of annual magistrates, a chosen senate, and the general assembly of the free inhabitants. Through this wise policy of non-interference, the City of London rapidly acquired wealth and importance, and before the evacuation of the island by the Romans, had attained a position of considerable grandeur. The civic institutions of the Saxons were, indeed, admirably suited for the adaptation of the municipal customs bequeathed to them by their predecessors, and which became developed to their full proportions through the greater amount of individual liberty that prevailed among the Germanic races.

Of the purely Teutonic institutions, one of the most characteristic was that of Gilds. Originally, a gild was nothing more than an association of ten families, for purposes of mutual protection and security. By the custom of "frankpledge," every freeman at the age of fourteen was called upon to give securities for his good behaviour. Gilds were therefore formed, binding themselves to produce the offender if any breach of the peace was committed by one of their members, or to give redress to the injured party. To carry out these objects a small fund was raised, to which every one contributed; and thence was derived the name of the association: "gildan," in Saxon, signifying to pay. With a view to becoming better acquainted with one another, and to draw more closely the bands of friendship, convivial meetings were held at fixed periods, when a vast quantity of beer was quaffed in honour of the living, and to the memory of the dead. In after-times this truly Saxon institution assumed greater proportions, and embraced both ecclesiastical and secular gilds. Of the former it is unnecessary to make further mention, but the latter formed the germ of the present livery companies. The earlier secular or mercantile gilds were associations of members of a particular trade or craft, for the purpose of maintaining and advancing the privileges of their peculiar calling. The term was also applied to a district or "soke," possessed of independent franchises, as in the case of the Portsoken Ward, which was anciently known as the Cnighten Gild. A "soke," or soca, it may be incidentally observed, was the territory in which was exercised the soca, or the privilege of hearing causes and disputes, levying fines, and administering justice within certain limits. The practice of gildating or embodying the aggregate free population of a town was of considerably later date. In France and in Flanders, corporations and communes, or commonalties, appear to have existed in the middle of the eleventh century, but the earliest mention of the Corporation of London occurs in the second year of the reign of Richard I. Availing himself of the king's absence in the Holy Land, his brother John, Earl of Moreton, anxious to acquire the co-operation of the city of London in his traitorous designs upon the crown, convened a general assembly of the citizens, and confirmed their ancient rights and privileges by a formal deed or charter. It was then, for the first time, that the commonalty of the city was regularly and officially recognized as a corporate body. The distinctive rights of a town corporation were the election of a council presided over by a mayor or bailiff, a common seal, a bell to convoke the citizens, and local jurisdiction.

But although it was not before the reign of Richard I. that the citizens of London were formed into a body corporate, they had enjoyed, as the inhabitants of a free burgh, the immunities and many essential privileges of a corporation, from the time of Edward the Confessor, if not of Alfred. Without stopping to discuss the etymology of the word "burgh," it may suffice to observe that at the period of the Conquest by far the greater part of the cities and towns of England were the private property of the king, or of some spiritual or secular lord, on whom they had been conferred by royal grant. These burghs, as they were called, were said to be held in demesne, and paid to their superior certain tolls, duties, and customs, levied on goods exposed for sale at markets and fairs. The inhabitants were actually little better than villeins or serfs, and were entirely at the mercy of their feudal lord. Immense, therefore, were the advantages possessed by the free burghs, such as London, which governed themselves, and compounded for all dues by the payment of a fixed annual sum. These annual contributions were styled the "farm," and, when perpetual, the burghs so compounding were said to be held at fee-farm of the king in capite, as was the case with London. One of the chief privileges implied by this tenure was that of exercising an independent jurisdiction, both civil and criminal, administered by magistrates chosen by the burgesses. It is supposed that criminal law was originally dispensed in the free gilds into which the city was divided, under the presidency of an alderman. These divisions were afterwards called wards, and were analogous to the corresponding division of the shire into hundreds. In each ward was held a court-leet, or ward-mote, dating from the time of Alfred, though the actual institution of wards by that name is no later than the reign of Edward I. Civil causes, in London at least, were tried before a peculiar tribunal, the president of which was probably the portreve, or, in minor causes, an alderman.

The Norman Conquest naturally suspended for a time all these privileges, and reduced all free towns to the level of burghs in demesne. Desirous, however, to secure the good will of the citizens, William hastened to assure them of his protection, and to confirm their prescriptive rights and immunities. Thus ran the gracious expression of the royal pleasure:—"William the king greets William the bishop, and Godfrey the portreve, and all the burghers within

London, French and English, friendly. And I make known to you that I will that ye be law-worthy, as ye were in the days of King Edward. And I will, that each child be his father's heir after his father's days. And I will not suffer that any man command you any wrong. God keep you."

The import of this charter was to make the citizens "free tenants," reserving to the king the seigniory, or proprietary title. The epithet "law-worthy" is equivalent to a declaration that they were freemen, for in the feudal ages none other were entitled to the forms of law; while the right of heirship apparently exempted them from the rule of primogeniture which prevailed among the Norman conquerors;—it is probable, however, that this exemption did not long hold good. In other respects the citizens of London continued to be governed by their own laws and usages, administered by their own magistrates after the ancient and established forms. A nucleus of liberty was thus preserved amidst the tyrannical usurpations of the Norman barons, and the bold burgesses many a time stoutly resisted the encroachments that were attempted to be made on their hereditary rights. At all periods of English history, indeed, have the citizens of London stepped forward as the champions of freedom, and shown themselves the incorruptible guardians of the public interests. Never at any time, however, was there greater necessity for a sturdy bulwark against the growing power of the oligarchy than at the present moment. Little by little—or, rather, by rapid strides—does the Government seek to get within its grasp the control of every department of the commonwealth. To-day, the East-India Company is abolished, for the sake of the "better government of India;" to-morrow, the Corporation is to be "reformed," for the "better government" of the City; the day after, some other long-established institution will be swept away. There is nothing so repugnant to a ministry as whatever savours of self-government; for how. in that case can the "Dowbs" be provided for? So long as the citizens manage their own affairs, there is no patronage at the disposal of ministers to bestow on a faithful or a wavering partisan. Young "honourables" and other needy scions of the governing classes have little ambition to undertake civic duties, while they are only onerous and expensive. Let the wedge be first applied. Let "reform" worm its way into the constitution of the Corporation, and then by degrees the whole edifice may gradually be subverted. Stipendiary magistracies and paid offices of any kind, if not too laborious, are always acceptable for sons, nephews, cousins, and influential supporters. The danger from this quarter is in truth greater than when Norman William had the island prostrate at his feet, and when the liberties of the City hung upon his word. That word went forth to save and to preserve. The stern warrior respected the rights of the industrious burgesses, and by his wisdom paved the way for the future greatness of the metropolis. But theoretical and doctrinaire statesmen are willing to risk all for the sake of consistency to certain arbitrary first principles, which do not apply to the spirit of the British people.

The charter of William the Conqueror, the reader will have remarked, alludes in a very general manner to the liberties and privileges enjoyed by the City. The first detailed and specific notice of their character occurs in the charter of Henry I. In the early part of his reign, being anxious to fix himself securely in his seat, the usurper conveyed, or confirmed, a grant to the citizens to hold Middlesex to farm for the yearly rental of 300 pounds; to appoint their own sheriff and their own justiciar; to be exempt from various burdensome and vexatious taxes in force in other parts of the kingdom; to be free from all denominations of tolls, customs, passage, and lestage, throughout the kingdom and along the seaboard; and to possess many other equally important privileges. This valuable charter was renewed by King Stephen, during whose stormy and troubled reign the metropolis enjoyed a degree of prosperity unknown to the rest of the kingdom. The comparative peace and security which distinguished the happy lot of the citizens of London, have been justly attributed to the maintenance of their ancient institutions, which may be said to have grown out of the habits, requirements, thoughts, and feelings characteristic of the Anglo-Saxon race. Nor were the Londoners unconscious of their power, or ungrateful to their benefactor. It was chiefly through their influence and exertions that the empress was finally driven out of the kingdom, and Stephen established on the throne. Henry II. confirmed the purport of preceding charters, and added some further immunities, concluding with the declaration that their ancient customs and liberties were to be held as of inheritance from the king and his heirs. They became, therefore, the property of the citizens, and were bequeathed from father to son, as a cherished heirloom. It is true that under Richard I. they were exposed to some extortion, for which they received ample amends during the reign of his weak and inglorious successor. Not only did they obtain five different charters confirmatory of their ancient privileges, together with the restoration of the sheriffwick, usurped by the last three monarchs, but also the first formal recognition of the mayoralty. These favours, however, did not render them untrue to the general interests of the nation, or betray them into a corrupt acquiescence with the absolute tendencies of the Crown. At that time, as at all others, while duly reverencing the royal prerogatives, they resolutely opposed themselves to the undue aggrandizement of the kingly power at the expense of the other estates of the realm. It was within the precincts of the City, at the metropolitan church of St. Paul's, that the articles of Magma Charta were first proposed and accepted by acclamation, the citizens binding themselves by oath to defend and enforce them with their lives. Nor was it for themselves alone that they were prepared to shed their blood. Their solicitude extended to all other cities and towns throughout the kingdom, for the preservation of whose free customs and immunities they expressly stipulated. During the long feeble reign of Henry III., no fewer than ten charters were granted to the citizens of London. In the thirty-first year of that monarch, the mayor and commonalty of the City of London are mentioned for the first time as a corporate body, possessing a common seal.

The reign of Edward I. was rendered memorable for the convocation of the first parliament of the freely-elected representatives of the people, for the purpose of voting the supplies necessary for the conduct of public affairs. Previously to this, grants of money were usually obtained through the personal influence of the barons over the cities and towns held in demesne. The burgesses, however, did not sit with the knights of shires, but apart by themselves, and, through loyalty or obsequiousness, assessed themselves in a contribution nearly one third greater than that granted by the barons and knights. The convenient precedent was not overlooked, and it became henceforth customary to expect the like liberality from subsequent parliaments. At this period, also, the principal divisions of the city were first denominated wards; these wards were presided over by an alderman, assisted by a council chosen by the inhabitants of each division. In the twelfth year of his reign, Edward, incensed by what he considered the disrespectful conduct of the civic magistrates, disfranchised the city, and governed it for twelve years through means of a custos. The experiment, however, did not answer, and the king was glad to restore the liberties of the City on payment of a heavy fine. At a later period, the mayor and sheriffs successfully resisted a second attempt to infringe on the privileges of the citizens. Under the second Edward, London continued to maintain its ascendancy over all the other cities in the kingdom, and it was now for the first time authentically ordained, that no person should be held to enjoy civic freedom unless he were a member of some trade or "mystery," or admitted by full assent of the commonalty assembled.

Two remarkable incidents marked the reign of Edward III. in connection with the City of London; the Lord Mayor was now constituted, by royal charter, one of the judges of oyer and terminer and gaol-delivery at Newgate. The ancient trading gilds also became developed into the present livery companies, so called, because a peculiar uniform was chosen by each. They were then likewise denominated crafts or mysteries, their president being styled a warden; the title of alderman being now reserved for the chief magistrates of wards. It may, too, be worthy of note that, in the 28th year of this reign the city serjeants received permission, when engaged in their official duties, and on great ceremonial occasions, to bear maces of gold or silver, with the royal or other arms thereon. We are told that this was considered a most flattering distinction, and that the mace-bearer, by virtue of his office, was deemed an esquire.

So gladly did our valiant and victorious kings of the olden times avail themselves of every opportunity to do honour to the liberality, courage, and fidelity of the wealthy and intelligent burgesses of London.

After various unsuccessful attempts to establish a representative form of government, it was at length decided, in the seventh year of Richard II., at a special convocation of the whole community of citizens, that there should be both a deliberative and an elective assembly. The latter, of course, consisted of the aggregate body of citizens, anciently designated immensa communitas, or folkmote, who were annually to elect four persons at the wardmote for each ward to represent the commonalty on all occasions of a deliberative nature. During the early part of this reign the City of London had no reason to complain of any lack of royal favour. Afterwards, however, Richard was guilty of many attempts at extortion, and even seized upon the franchises of the City, on the pretext of a riot, notwithstanding that the first charter of his grandfather, Edward III., had debarred such forfeiture as the consequence of individual misconduct. These acts of oppression very naturally and justly alienated the attachment of the Londoners, and prepared them to give a hearty welcome to Bolingbroke. This good-feeling was maintained throughout the reign of Henry IV., who testified his gratitude by the grant of several valuable privileges. A like cordial understanding between the citizens and their sovereign existed under Henry V., and the City, in consequence, increased in opulence, population, and influence. Guildhall was built, and the streets were lighted at night by public lanterns. The halcyon days, however, of the City of London must be referred to the reign of the fourth Edward. The citizens never wavered in their attachment to his fortunes, nor did that gay and gallant monarch ever exhibit any coldness of feeling — at least, towards their fair dames. Of Richard III. it is unnecessary to speak, and even of Henry VII there is little to be said, save that he never omitted an opportunity of fleecing the citizens and replenishing his exchequer.

Under Henry VIII. the City of London earned the honourable distinction of being the only body of men in the realm who dared to resist the king's systematic abuse of the royal power. Henry had revived the unconstitutional practice of imposing taxes without the consent of the Commons; but the citizens opposed his illegal demands with such resolution that he was compelled to desist for the time and to proceed with greater caution for the future. Another distinguishing feature of this reign was the profuse extravagance of the citizens on ceremonial occasions. The chronicles of the period teem with marvellous descriptions of the pomp and pageantry displayed whenever a royal or illustrious personage honoured the City with a visit. In modern times this semi-barbarous love of ostentation has been superseded by a genial and dignified hospitality, that has tended in no slight degree to increase the fame and influence of that important quarter of the metropolis. Each successive sovereign of this great empire has accepted with grateful pride the magnificent demonstrations of loyalty tendered by the faithful burgesses. Foreign potentates and ambassadors have equally deemed it an honour to receive the congratulations of these princely traders at their sumptuous banquets, celebrated throughout the world. The ministers of the day feel their position to be insecure until it has been ratified by the acclamations of the citizens, and the hospitable attentions of the civic magistrates. Statesmen and warriors, poets and historians, men of thought and men of action, are all stimulated to exertion by the honourable hope of being distinguished by the burgesses of London, and enrolled in the lists of freemen. On such occasions the city magnates hold high festival, and by their graceful hospitality inspire every breast with generous sympathy. Formal and priggish persons are said to exist who object to the cost of such entertainments, and, in the spirit of Judas, ask why, instead of purchasing these dainty cates, the money is not distributed among the poor. Is it possible that they do not perceive that every farthing spent on these stately banquets finds its way into general circulation, benefiting almost every branch of trade, and giving employment to thousands of artisans? To hear them speak, one would suppose that the cook and the butler alone profited by such occasions, whereas it is strictly and literally true that not a single gala takes place in the City without the circulating medium percolating through every warehouse, magazine, shop, and stall within the Bills of Mortality. Independently of this consideration, these civic feasts are symbols of those great old Saxon institutions which have made England the home and guardian of liberty. Our hearty and large-souled ancestors never dreamed of weighing every miserable coin, or of stinting the measure of their generous wines or foaming ale. They gave not less to the poor because they delighted to honour the brave and good, or to greet one another in the loving cup. Unlike the coldly intellectual reformers and theorists of the present day, they did not consider the gaol and the workhouse as the only asylums for poverty. They were men of feeling and kindly impulse, not of abstract principles. They gave their cheerful alms to the mendicants, and spread a bounteous board for their neighbours. Fools that they were! How is it that they did not recognize the mendicant to be an impostor and a drone, or bethink them that the money with which they feasted their neighbour might have purchased a field? It was because they were warm-hearted, warm-blooded men, and not mere calculating machines. They were glorious creatures, with thews and sinews, and they made their country great and powerful among the nations of the world; but they never paused to denounce the cost of a dinner, or to grudge a flowing bowl to their kinsfolk and neighbours. Besides, our Pharisees of reform conveniently forget that the copious banquets at which they turn up their envious eyes are mostly defrayed from private funds. The sheriffs, for instance, derive no aid from public moneys; their own fortunes provide the means for handsomely entertaining friends and strangers, and for dispensing open-handed charity. The Lord Mayor himself almost invariably draws upon his own resources to a large amount, in order to maintain the ancient reputation and actual present influence of the City of London. Demolish Gog and Magog, put down the civic banquets, break up and melt down the weighty and many-linked chains of solid gold round the neck of my lord mayor and the sheriffs, strip off the aldermen's gowns, make a bonfire of the gilded carriages, wring, if you will, the necks of both swans and cygnets. It is all vanity and vexation. Man is an intellectual animal: he wants none of these gewgaws. Alas! Wisdom may cry aloud in the streets, but no one will heed her words if she speaks beyond his comprehension. In theory, these Pecksniffs of retrenchment might possibly be correct if mankind had attained the same degree of marble indifference with themselves. In the mean time, while we are honest and true, it is good to be merry and wise.

Passing lightly over the intervening reigns, we now arrive at that of James I., who granted three very valuable charters to the Corporation of London. The first alludes to the immemorial right of the mayor and commonalty to the conservancy of the Thames, and to the metage of all coals, grain, salt, fruit, vegetables, and other merchandise sold by measure, delivered at the port of London. Of the exact nature of these privileges and of their beneficial operation, so far as public interests are concerned, we shall have occasion to speak hereafter, merely premising in this place that they have been enjoyed "from time whereof the memory of man runneth not to the contrary." The second charter, after confirming former liberties, enlarges the limits of the civic jurisdiction and ordains that the mayor, recorder, and two aldermen, shall be justices of oyer and terminer. The third one is simply an amplification of the preceding two, and clears up various doubts as to the weighing and measuring of coals: both offices are granted or confirmed.

The tyrannical and oppressive treatment of the citizens of London by Charles I. is too well known to need more than a passing allusion. Not only did he imprison the aldermen for refusing to act dishonourably towards their fellow-citizens; not only did he make illegal demands and impose arbitrary fines, but he even deprived them of the right of petition and remonstrance. Such despotic conduct could not do otherwise than alienate the affection of those who had previously displayed many proofs of their loyalty to the Crown and attachment to the royal person. The City consequently made common cause with the Parliament, freely expending both blood and treasure in defence of the national freedom. Who has mot read with kindling cheeks how the bold 'prentices, armed only with spears, withstood a furious charge of the fiery Rupert at the head of his gallant cavaliers? But though prepared to resist the abuse of the royal prerogative, the citizens were not disposed to transfer their allegiance to a usurper, who, in the name of liberty, trampled liberty under foot. Accordingly we find them consistently opposed to the military absolutism of Cromwell, and among the first to co-operate with Monk in effecting the restoration to the throne of the royal line of Stuart.

The Stuarts, however, like the Bourbons, were incapable of benefiting by the lessons of adversity. It was not long before "the merry monarch" was involved in most unmirthful disputes with the citizens, whom he endeavoured to deprive of their ancient right to elect their own sheriffs. For the moment he partially succeeded, and, encouraged by this success, formed the design of seizing the charters of every corporate borough in the kingdom. The chief difficulty rested with London: if that could be overcome, the smaller cities would fall an easy prey. The law officers of the Crown were accordingly instructed to make out a case to sanction the forfeiture of the city charters. A double pretext was soon invented. It was stated that nine years before, the Common Council had levied a new scale of tolls on the public markets rebuilt after the great fire, and at a more recent period had printed a libellous petition impugning the king's justice. On these slender pleas a writ of quo warranto was taken out against the City, and the judges, under the undoubted influence of the Court, pronounced sentence of forfeiture, although a charter of the 7th Richard II. expressly provides against any forfeiture of the City's liberties notwithstanding any abuse of them whatsoever. This exhibition of violence so terrified the other corporations of the kingdom, that most of them at once tendered the surrender of their franchises, with the ignominious hope of obtaining better terms for themselves. James II. walked in the steps of his brother, and showed even greater determination to destroy the liberties of the nation. The disaffection of his subjects and the landing of the Prince of Orange warned him, when too late, that he had gone too far. Anxious to make friends in his hour of extremest peril, he despatched the infamous Jefferies to Guildhall to announce the restoration of the ancient privileges of the City. But the citizens were not thus to be cajoled. No sooner had the king set out to join his forces, than the Court of Aldermen declared themselves in favour of the Prince of Orange, as the champion of civil and religious freedom. The Lord Mayor, the aldermen, and fifty common councillors, had a seat and voice in the convention which pronounced the deposition of James, and the elevation to the throne of William and Mary. The first act of the nation was to establish and perpetuate a constitutional form of government, and this was accomplished by passing the famous statute known as the Bill of Rights. Experience had proved the vital importance of placing the privileges of the City of London beyond the caprice of the sovereign and the possibility of a coup d'etat. It was therefore declared by Parliament that the judgment passed on the quo warranto of Charles II. was unjust and illegal, and that all the proceedings in the case were informal and void. It was further enacted, "that the mayor, commonalty, and citizens, should for ever thereafter remain a body corporate and politic, without any seizure or forejudger, or being thereof excluded or ousted, upon any pretence of forfeiture or misdemeanour whatsoever, theretofore or thereafter to be done, committed, or suffered." The constitution of the corporation was nevertheless subsequently violated by the statute of 11 Geo. I., which conferred on the livery the elective franchises exercised in common hall. By a still more recent act, 12 & 13 Victoria, the right of voting in the election of aldermen and common councilmen has been further extended and enlarged. It was then enacted that that privilege should belong to every freeman of the City rated at 10 pounds per annum to the police or any other rate, and registered among the voters for the city of London at elections of members to serve in Parliament. Still greater innovations are now in contemplation, in violation of law and usage, and in defiance of prescriptive right, royal charters, and parliamentary statutes.

Audax omnia perpeti, Gens humana ruit per vetitum nefas.*

* The materials for this slight sketch have been gathered from
Norton's "History and Franchises of the City of London;" Dr. Brad-
y's
learned dissertation on Boroughs; and Herbert's "History of the
Twelve
Livery Companies."

PART I.

THE CORPORATION AS IT IS.

The Municipal Constitution — Lord Mayor — Aldermen — Court of Common
Council — Citizens — The Livery Companies — Sheriffs — Law Courts — Public
Charities — Conservancy of the Thames — Metage Dues.

In the preceding hasty sketch it has been attempted to trace the rise of London from being the bazaar to a Roman camp to its present position as the capital of the commercial world. It is now worth while to glance at the nature of the municipal institutions through which it has attained such a proud ascendancy.*

* The authority chiefly consulted for the following statements is Pulling's "Practical Treatise on the Laws, Customs, Usages, and Regulations of the City and Port of London."

Strictly speaking, London cannot be said to possess any original charter, or specific definition of its rights and franchises. Those conferred since the Conquest, without exception, allude directly or indirectly to preceding documents of a similar nature. In fact the customs and usages of the City grew out of the ancient Saxon institutions, grafted, as they were, on the Roman municipal stock. The City of London represents a county, and as such is divided into hundreds, called wards; each having its own wardmote, presided over by its own alderman. The Lord Mayor, the Court of Aldermen, and the Court of Common Council, together with the incorporated guilds which elect the civic magistrates, form the municipal constitution.

In ancient times the chief civic magistrate was styled the Reve, or Portreve, but in 1207 John changed this title to that of Mayor. The appellation of Lord was first prefixed in the fourth charter of Edward III., when the honour of having gold or silver maces borne before him was conferred on the "Lord Mayor," who ranked moreover as an earl. His duties are multiplex and ubiquitous. In his own person he represents all the rights and privileges of the Corporation. He is said to hold the same relation to the City as the Crown does to the rest of the kingdom. He is chief butler at the coronation of the sovereign, lord-lieutenant of the county of London, clerk of the markets, gauger of wine and oil, meter of coals and grain, salt and fruit, conservator of the Thames, admiral of the port, justice of gaol delivery for Newgate, chairman of every committee he attends, and subject to many other burdens. The election of Lord Mayor takes place on the 29th September, when the livery usually nominate the two senior aldermen who have not passed the chair; of these the senior is generally chosen by the Court of Aldermen. The chain of office is then placed round his neck, and he himself presented to the Lord Chancellor. He does not, however, immediately enter upon his important duties, but remains in a chrysalis form, under the title of Lord Mayor elect, until the 8th of November, when he takes the oath of office, at the Guildhall, and on the following day is present-ed to the Barons of the Exchequer, at Westminster, for the confirma-tion of the Crown. The annual salary is 8,000 pounds, which rarely suffices to meet the incessant demands on the Lord Mayor's charity and hospitality. He is expected to contribute to every charitable institution within his jurisdiction, and to a great many beyond it, and to head every subscription for praiseworthy purposes. His pri-vate alms also amount to a very large sum, and his hospitality is proverbial. He represents, in short, the best phase of the old feudal baron, or rather of the Saxon eorl, exercising a paternal and benefi-cient supervision over all who reside within the limits of his author-ity.

The Aldermen.

Among the Anglo-Saxons the title of alderman was regarded as one of the most honourable distinctions to which a freeman could aspire. After a time, however, it was conferred with somewhat too liberal courtesy on nearly every individual vested with authority. The presidents of district guilds were especially known by this des-ignation, which they afterwards monopolized when the guilds be-came raised into wards or hundreds of the city. The aldermen then partially recovered their former dignity, and in the charter of Henry I. are mentioned as barons. The position and authority of an alderman, though they have much declined since the olden times, are still a reasonable object of ambition. He is a justice of the peace, as well as the presiding officer of his ward, and, by virtue of his office, a member of the Court of Common Council; but it is rather in their collective than their individual capacity that their power and usefulness are most conspicuous. Independently of their judicial duties, the Court of Aldermen constitute the executive department of the Corporation; with them rests the cognizance of the return of every civic officer elected at a wardmote court, and also of the election of common-councillors. They swear in brokers and other officers, and investigate the validity of claims to civic freedom. For the proper discharge of these and similar duties, they are singularly adapted through their local knowledge, which is likewise of material service to her Majesty's judges at the Central Criminal Court. This circumstance further renders them most efficient as city magistrates,—far more so, indeed, than any police or stipendiary magistrate could ever hope to be. Personally acquainted with the inhabitants of their respective wards, they are in a position to obtain peculiar and authentic information as to the characters, habits, and motives of witnesses, accusers, and accused. Their devotion to public business is wholly disinterested, for there are no pecuniary emoluments attached to the office, which has truly little to recommend it, save as being a sphere of active utility, and as a gratifying token of the good-will of one's fellow-citizens. The proper style of the Court is the "Court of the Mayor and Aldermen in the Inner Chamber." It consists of the Lord Mayor or his deputy—an alderman who has passed the chair—and not less than twelve other aldermen. The proceedings of the Court are entered in journals called "Repertories," which are kept in the muniment-room. The Recorder, the Steward of Southwark, the Clerk to the Lord Mayor, the keepers, governors, chaplains, and surgeons of the different prisons, and other officers of the Corporation, are elected by this Court, which, for assiduity, intelligence, and incorruptibility, yields to no body of men in the kingdom.

Court of Common Council.

But however distinguished may be the civic position, however great the moral influence, of the Lord Mayor and the Court of Aldermen, the controlling power is, after all, centred in the Common

Council. At a very remote period the freemen of the City were accustomed to meet in general assembly, and to act as one body. As their numbers increased, the many inconveniences of such a mode of proceeding soon became manifest; and so early as the reign of the first Edward representatives began to be chosen from each ward for the despatch of real business. At first the guilds, or trading companies, claimed the right of election as their exclusive privilege, and consequently excited the jealousy of the mass of the inhabitants. It was therefore arranged that the men of each guild or "mystery" should choose their own delegates from among themselves, and this was the more easily accomplished, as at that time each craft occupied a separate quarter, as is still the custom in the East. This arrangement, however, was of brief duration, and a more permanent settlement was effected in the reign of Richard II. It was then agreed that every ward should annually elect four of the most efficient persons in the ward to sit in the Common Council for the following year, and whose names should be presented to the mayor — that high functionary being charged to accept no more than eight members of any one "mystery" for the whole city. As the wards varied in extent and population, it was further agreed that the larger wards should return six councillors, and the smaller four or two, according to their sufficiency. The number of the Common Council was then fixed at 96 members, but gradually increased to the present number of 206, who are chosen as follows:-

Bassishaw and Lime Street each return 4; Dowgate, Candlewick, Cordwainers, Cornhill, Queenhithe, Vintry, and Walbrook, 6; Bread Street, Bridge, Billingsgate, Broad Street, Cheap, Coleman Street, Cripplegate Within, and Cripplegate Without, Tower, Langbourn, Castle Baynard, Aldersgate, Aldgate, and Portsoken, 8; Bishopsgate and Farringdon-within, 14; and Farringdon-without, 16. These true representatives of the citizens constitute the Court of Common Council, under the style and title of "Court of the Lord Mayor, Aldermen, and Commoners of the City of London in Common Council assembled." It requires the presence of the Lord Mayor, or his deputy — an alderman who has passed the chair — two aldermen and thirty-eight common councilmen, to make a quorum. There are usually twelve ordinary meetings in the year, and on an average thirteen extraordinary meetings, convened for special purposes by a requisition to the Lord Mayor signed by seven members. The proceedings are conducted as nearly as possible according to the routine of the House of Commons, and embrace a vast variety of subjects of local and sometimes national importance. The Court has a double function — legislative and executive. In the former capacity it enacts by-laws for the better government of the Corporation, in conformity with immemorial usage confirmed by 15 Edward III., and again more recently and fully by the Municipal Corporations Act. The charter of Edward III. authorizes the mayor and aldermen, with the assent of the commonalty, "where any customs theretofore used and obtained proved hard or defective, or any matters newly arising within the City needed amendment, and no remedy had been previously provided, to apply and ordain a convenient remedy, as often as it should seem expedient; so that the same were agreeable to good faith and reason, for the common advantage of the citizens, and other liege subjects sojourning with them, and useful to king and people." Vested with such powers as these, the Corporation of London are clearly competent to introduce whatever reforms circumstances may render desirable. As practical men of business, the Court of Common Council may fairly be supposed to be the best judges as to the nature of the amendments to be made, and the right time of making them. Persons engaged in commercial pursuits are not usually obstructive, or opposed to useful innovations. On the contrary, being wedded to no theories, they are constantly impelled to change, and to act upon each emergency as it arises. The past history of the City of London is one long illustration of this position, — it is an uninterrupted series of reforms, many of them rather beneficial to the nation at large than to the Corporation itself. On what grounds, then, is it justifiable to supersede this salutary internal action of the Corporation, and to exercise the arbitrary power of the legislature to enforce crude and inapplicable innovations? This interference with the self-government of the City is, in fact, a vote of censure on the duly elected representatives of the citizens, with whom the majority of the citizens themselves are, however, perfectly satisfied. But, in truth, that "self-government" is the head and front of their offence, for is it not a stumbling-block to ministerial and oligarchical influence? In addition to the power of enacting by-laws, the Common Council superintend the disposal of the funds of the Corporation; and without their previous consent no larger sum than 100 pounds can be paid for any purpose whatsoever. Their executive functions are also considerable. Upon this court depends the responsibility of electing the common serjeant, the town clerk, the two judges, and officers of the Sheriffs' Court, the clerk of the peace, the coroner, the remembrancer, the commissioner of the city police, and various other officers of inferior note and standing.

The Citizens.

The "complete" citizen may be defined as a ten-pound householder, paying scot and bearing lot. The freedom of the City is not, however, attainable by simple residence. It is to be acquired only by three modes—by patrimony, by apprenticeship, or by redemption. A royal charter, even, is insufficient to make the grantee free of the City. The freedom of the City is not confined to the male sex. Free-women are called free sisters, but cannot transmit their freedom, which is, moreover, suspended during coverture. Freedom by service is acquired by a seven years' apprenticeship to a freeman or freewoman, the indenture being enrolled at the Chamberlain's office within twelve months of its execution. The apprentice need not necessarily be articled to a member of any guild, fraternity, or trading company, but he must not be the son of an alien. Freedom by redemption, or purchase, is of a threefold nature:—1st. It may take the form of a fine for any breach of the apprenticeship indentures; 2nd. It is often bestowed as an honorary distinction on individuals eminent for their public services; and 3rd. Admission to the freedom of the City is by presentment by persons entitled to confer that privilege. It is imperative on all persons elected to a corporate office, or "occupying premises and carrying on any trade, business, or profession, within the City and its liberties," to become free of the City. This is done by the payment of the fees of the officers and of 5 pounds to the Corporation. The advantages of the freedom, though not so great in the present day as in ancient times, are still considerable. Besides being a bond of union and mutual protection, it entitles its possessor to a vote at the elections of the aldermen and the common council of the ward. Only freemen can act as brokers, or, indeed, carry on any trade within the boundaries of the City.

The Companies.

As the City of London waxed mighty and opulent, proportionate was the increase of the wealth and importance of its component parts. The humble guilds or crafts gradually developed themselves into large and influential trading companies, to belong to which was deemed an honour not beneath the consideration of royalty. Edward III., for instance, did not disdain to be enrolled in the Worshipful Company of Linen Armourers, now Merchant Tailors; and his example was followed by his successor, Richard II. The example, indeed, was contagious, for in the reign of the latter monarch the company in question could boast of the fellowship of four royal dukes, ten earls, ten barons, and five bishops. The custom has come down to our own times, and the proudest names in the aristocracy are recorded in the books of the City companies. The presidents of these crafts or mysteries were styled Wardens, who were assisted by a small number of delegates of the guild in presenting to the City Chamberlain all defaults against the rules and ordinances of the mystery. These companies were not all equally regarded by either the sovereign or the citizens. Towards the close of the reign of Edward II. the more important companies separated from the less wealthy; and this distinction was soon so far recognized, that precedency was given to the following twelve companies:- 1. Mercers; 2. Grocers; 3. Drapers; 4. Fishmongers; 5. Goldsmiths; 6. Skinners; 7. Merchant Tailors; 8. Haberdashers; 9. Salters; 10. Ironmongers; 11. Vintners; 12. Cloth workers. In these companies the freemen from early times have been of two classes; the upper, entitled to wear the "livery" or uniform of the company; and the lower, consisting mostly of workmen. The representatives of the companies were chosen from the former, and are mentioned in the charters as probi homines. In the fifteenth year of Edward IV. the Common Council enacted, that the masters, wardens, and probi homines of the several mysteries should repair to the Guildhall in their last liveries, for the purpose of electing the Lord Mayor, sheriffs, and other civic officers; and that the members of the Common Council should be the only other persons present. This court now consists of the Lord Mayor or his deputy—an alderman who has passed the chair—four aldermen, and the liverymen of the companies who are also freemen. Their office is to elect the Lord Mayor, sheriffs, chamberlain, bridge-master, and auditors of the City and Bridge-house accounts, and the four ale-conners. The official style of the court is, "A Meeting or Assembly of the Mayor, Aldermen, and Liverymen of the several Companies of the City of London in Common Hall assembled." The franchise is confined to liverymen of a year's standing, who have paid their livery fines in full, without receiving any drawback or allowance. The mode of proceeding is by a show of hands, but a poll may be demanded by any of the candidates, or by two electors.

The Sheriffs.

The office of Sheriff has somewhat fallen from its ancient "high estate." According to Stow, they were formerly "the mayor's eyes, seeing and supporting part of the case, which the person of the mayor is not alone sufficient to bear." In olden times the sheriffs were always conjoined with the mayor and aldermen in proclamations requiring them to preserve the peace of the City. From a very remote period the right of electing these officers belonged to the citizens, and later charters acknowledge and confirm the privilege. Henry I. granted to them to hold Middlesex to farm, for 300 pounds a year, and to appoint their own sheriff; while the second charter of John confirms to them the sheriffwick of London and Middlesex at the rent or farm of 300 pounds, "blank sterling money," and declares that they "shall make amongst themselves sheriffs whom they will, and remove them when they will." In those times this was a very important privilege, for the sheriff, or shire-reve, as the king's bailiff, was possessed of extraordinary powers, which he usually exercised in a very corrupt and oppressive manner. The sheriffs of London are the sheriff of Middlesex; in the former capacity they are addressed in the plural, in the latter in the singular. Though shorn of its beams, the office of Sheriff is still a highly honourable one, nor are the duties light or unimportant which devolve upon these functionaries. The honour, moreover, is as costly as it is onerous; not only do the sheriffs receive no salary, but they are conventionally expected to disburse several thousand pounds in charities and hospitality. The inspection of the city gaols occupies no small portion of their time, nor do they enjoy much intermission from the incessant demands for eleemosynary aid. That an office so costly and troublesome should be an object of competition, is certainly a striking proof of the disinterested and patriotic spirit of the citizens of London.

The Law Courts.

With characteristic love of fair play, our ancestors laid it down as a leading principle, that "justice should be administered at every man's own door, in the presence of his neighbours." It is, indeed, a primary element of good government, that the dispensation of justice should be prompt and inexpensive, and without favour of persons. With the exception of the City of London, however, and a few other privileged places, the local tribunals were gradually superseded through the centralizing action of the superior courts. But even in London the civic franchises have been seriously diminished through the ruling of those courts that the privilege claimed by the citizens to be sued only before their own local tribunals is confined to real, and does not extend to transitory actions.

The highest court of civic judicature was the Hustings Court, so called from the Saxon word hustings, signifying the "house of things," or causes. It was presided over by the Lord Mayor and Sheriffs, but the proceedings were actually conducted, and judgment pronounced, by the Recorder. All real and mixed cases, saving ejectment, fell within the province of this court, which was held at Guildhall on every alternate Tuesday. This court, however, though not formally abolished, does not now sit, and all the business formerly transacted at it is transferred to the Lord Mayor Court and the City Small Debts Court. In ancient times, the registration of deeds, wills, and titles to land, belonged also to this court, and the record in the Hustings of a sale or purchase of lands was deemed a sufficient voucher. It has been suggested that, as the necessity of a proper system of registration of the sale or mortgage of real property is becoming daily more evident, the machinery for accomplishing that purpose is afforded by the Court of Hustings, so far, at least, as the City is concerned. Practically, the most important court, however, at the present day, is the Lord Mayor's Court, or Court of Aldermen of the Outer Chamber. As in the Hustings Court, the actual judge is the Recorder, though the Lord Mayor and Aldermen are supposed to preside. In some respects, this court is one of equity, with the advantage over the Court of Chancery of being at the same time more expeditious, quite as equitable, and far less expensive. As a court of common law, it takes cognizance of all personal and mixed actions, without exception, and in its operations and bearings is altogether a striking example of the benefits incidental to local self-government. The Sheriffs' Court of the City of London for the recovery of small debts is also admirably adapted to the requirements of a free commercial people, and is of inestimable value to the small tradesmen of London.

Public Charities.

The monastic institutions in Roman Catholic countries provide for, and thereby foster, a large amount of idle and reckless habits. Previous to the Reformation, this was certainly the case in England. Not only the sick, the maimed, and the accidentally necessitous were fed and clothed,—the same indiscriminating charity was extended to those far less worthy of the sympathy of their fellow-creatures. On the suppression of conventual establishments, it would have fared badly with the deserving poor in London had not the Corporation stepped forward to help them. At present, the princely sum of 10,000 pounds is annually disbursed from the corporate funds in contributions to various hospitals, asylums, schools, dispensaries, and local charities; but even this large sum of money would be inadequate to the purpose, were it not supplemented by the individual munificence of the citizens. The Lord Mayor, the Sheriffs, the Aldermen, and the other civic dignitaries vie with one another in an open-handed liberality, which asks no other condition than that the recipient shall actually stand in need of aid, and be worthy of relief and assistance. It is much to be feared, however, that with the declining influence of the Corporation, the stream of private charity will also dry up. The continued payment of the 10,000 pounds a year may, indeed, be secured by Act of Parliament; but no Act of Parliament can alter human nature. Proud of their position as the chosen delegates and representatives of their fellow-citizens, among whom they and their fathers have lived for generations, the City potentates have, of their abundance, contributed lavishly and without stint to every local institution deserving of sympathy and support. And not only these, but the livery companies likewise have given lordly amounts to charitable establishments both within and without the City liberties, and have founded schools in many distant parts of the kingdom. But if the Corporation is to be "reformed" after the manner of Sir George Grey and his coadjutors—if the esprit de corps, which is now so beneficially and beneficently exhibited, is to be suppressed, what reasonable hope remains that men who have been arbitrarily deprived of all real interest in City matters will still devote their time, their energies, and their fortunes to purposes which only remunerate them with toil, anxiety, and personal discomfort? The inevitable tendency of the proposed Bill is to reduce the entire administration of the City to a dull, heartless routine. Step by step the continental system of home government is being insinuated into this hitherto free country. Yet a few years of unchecked progress in that direction, and it will be proposed to appoint crown officers to preside over county and town, city and borough. The approaches to absolute power, under the less alarming title of centralization, though insidious, have long been apparent to all who study the workings of system-mongers. Unless a vigorous stand be now made against these continued encroachments of ministerial and oligarchical influence, the middle classes will, ere long, have to content themselves with being literally a "nation of shopkeepers," without any object of honourable ambition in view, without any hope of obtaining distinction and eminence in the annals of their country, and reduced to the one narrow pursuit of "making money." Are the free burgesses of London prepared thus to sacrifice their birthright to gratify the whim or envy of a Whig ex-minister?

Conservancy of the Thames.

To the disciples of the modern doctrine that ancient charters were given only to be abolished, and parliamentary statutes enacted only to be repealed, it is idle to state that the first charter of James I. acknowledged that the conservation of the water of the Thames had been held time out of mind by the mayor and commonalty. Those, however, who still reverence the ancient landmarks, and regard with respect the honest feelings and manly wisdom of their ancestors, will not treat so lightly claims derived from immemorial usage and prescriptive right. >From time, then, "whereof the memory of man runneth not to the contrary," the conservancy of the Thames has been one of the duties and privileges of the mayoralty of the City of London. The jurisdiction of the Thames conservator extends from Staines Bridge to Yendall or Yenleet, and from Colemouth Creek to Cockham Wood in the Medway, including every bank, shore, and wharf within those limits. The duties of the office are to remove all wears and other obstructions, to prevent the construction of piers or wharfs calculated to impede the navigation of the river, to protect the fisheries, and generally to take care that neither the channel nor the banks suffer injury through the malice or heedlessness of individuals, or from accidental causes. This department of the corporate administration is at present intrusted to the Navigation Committee, annually selected from the Court of Common Council, who make periodical excursions on the river, and judge with their own eyes as to what is desirable to be done or avoided. No doubt these functions could be discharged by a government officer, the friend or relative of a man of parliamentary influence, and equally without doubt this consideration is likely to carry more weight in the House of Commons than any claims derived from immemorial usage and centuries of beneficial operation.

The Metage Dues.

The same charter of James I. which confirmed the ancient right of the mayor and commonalty of London to the conservation of the water of the Thames, declares that the citizens are equally, and on the same grounds, entitled to exercise the office of measuring all coals, cereals, fruits, vegetables, salt, and other merchandise sold by measure, brought to the port of London. In the beginning, this privilege arose out of the necessity of ascertaining the exact quantity of these articles actually imported into the City, in order fairly to collect the king's customs. It has since been found mutually beneficial to all parties that all measurable goods should be meted out by sworn meters, carefully selected for their responsible duties, and over whom is maintained a constant and jealous supervision. The Court of Common Council appoint ten "corn-meters in trust," who are placed over 150 deputy meters, chosen by the Corn and Coal and Finance Committee, and sworn in the Lord Mayor's Court to do their duty without fear or favour. There are also a few other officers connected with this very important branch of the civic regulations as to trade, to whom, however, it is unnecessary further to allude than as an illustration of the useful and practical precautions adopted by the Corporation to secure strict fairness of dealing between buyer and seller. The fruit-meters are four in number, who appoint their own deputies, and are equally bound to impartiality. There are likewise twenty-one deputy oyster-meters, one salt-meter and several deputies, and a fruit-shifter and a salt-shifter. It is now proposed to deprive the Corporation of the funds realized by these metage dues. The principle of free trade is to be carried out to an extent that will exclude honesty as an essential ingredient in commercial transactions. Everything, we are told, finds its own level. Every man is the best guardian of his own interests. Neither seller nor buyer will submit to be wronged by the other. It is contrary to the modern system of trade to interfere between dealers and purchasers; they are quite competent to take care of themselves, and are quite ready to dispense with the intervention of a third party. Besides, there is no necessity to do away with sworn meters, payable by the job according to a fixed scale. The only alteration that is required is the confiscation of the right of the Corporation to derive any profit from their labours. This doctrine of confiscation is a convenient one, but it is somewhat inconsistent with the outcry that has so recently been raised because Lord Canning was supposed to have confiscated the rights of certain farmers of the revenue in India; for that is the exact position of a talookdar. Now the Corporation farms, and has from time out of mind farmed, the revenue arising from these various sources. The sovereign is the seignior of the City, and therefore entitled in the first instance to all customs, duties, revenues, and imposts levied within its precincts. But on various grounds, and by various means, — such as petition, purchase, composition, and extraordinary services — the citizens of London have at various times obtained the remission or enjoyment of these different sources of income. The metage dues are therefore as much their property as an hereditary estate is that of its acknowledged proprietor. Their title to these dues is of considerably longer standing than that of his Grace the Duke of Bedford to Woburn Abbey, and those of so many lay impropriators of church property. If royal charters and Acts of Parliament are of no greater value than waste paper, there is of course nothing more to be said on the subject. There is nothing, then, to oppose as a barrier to any act of spoliation. Blackstone, indeed, says that Parliament is omnipotent to bind or to loose, and competent to annul charters and to repeal its own statutes. It is certainly no new thing for Parliament to stultify itself, but it is also certain that the Legislature will better consult its reputation by occasionally repressing its eagerness to cancel the proceedings of its predecessors, and by abstaining from too frequent indulgence in acts of confiscation.

The coal duties, however, demand a fuller consideration than any other department of City finance. The first charter of Richard II. confirmed to the Corporation of London "the custody" of the persons and property of all orphans. According to ancient custom, the citizens could dispose by will of only one-third of their personal estate, the remaining two-thirds being paid into the Court of Orphans in trust for their children. A very large sum of money was at times thus invested, to the no small advantage of all parties concerned in the arrangement. But in the seventeenth century the Corporation became involved in debt to this fund, and to private individuals, to the extent of three-quarters of a million sterling. This state of bankruptcy was by no means the result of imprudence or ostentatious extravagance. During the Rebellion the City had been despoiled by both parties under various pretexts. After the Restoration the great fire consumed a vast amount of city property and necessitated a ruinous outlay in the reconstruction of entire streets. To this was added the shutting up of the Exchequer by Charles II., and the seizure of the charter when the City refused any longer to provide the means for his selfish and disgraceful prodigality. A better era, however, was inaugurated by the accession of William and Mary, in the fifth and sixth of whose reign an Act was passed for raising what was called an "Orphans' Fund." The estates of the Corporation were charged with the annual payment of 8,000 pounds towards the liquidation of their debt, and for the same purpose a duty of 2,000 pounds a year on the personal property of the citizens was paid till 1795. To meet these heavy charges a duty of fourpence per chaldron was levied on coals and culm imported into London, and also an additional duty of sixpence per chaldron for fifty years. By this means the debt of 750,000 pounds was finally discharged in 1782, but another debt had been contracted by the Corporation being called upon to contribute to public improvements beyond the just limits of their jurisdiction. By the year 1823 no less a sum than 846,300 pounds had been expended in this manner out of the Orphans' Fund, and in the l0th of George IV. a further sum of 1,000,000 pounds was charged upon the fund to defray the expenses for improving the approaches to London Bridge. Under

William IV., however, the coal duties were fixed at one shilling per ton in lieu of metage, and an additional one penny per ton was allowed for the expenses of the market. This statute extends to a circle measured by a radius of twenty miles from the General Post-office, and up to the present time has been productive of much good to the general interests of the entire metropolis. A duty upon coals is naturally unpopular, and it would be difficult to devise one that was otherwise. It is always easy to raise a popular clamour against taxes that press upon matters of first necessity, but in what other way is the public exchequer to be replenished? It will not suffice to tax objects of luxury alone, and with regard to the coal duty it is very improbable that the poor would benefit in the slightest degree by its repeal. The utmost reduction in the price of coals that could be expected, would be a little more than a halfpenny per hundredweight, and this difference is far more likely to find its way into the pocket of the vender than into that of the needy purchaser. There is, moreover, another trifling consideration to be taken into account before the abolition of these duties be decided upon. Relying on the respect usually paid to property in this country, and confiding in the good faith of the House of Commons, the Corporation have mortgaged these duties in order to raise a very large sum of money. It was not for any purposes of civic ostentation, or indeed for any purely civic object, that they were induced to incur this heavy obligation. Cannon Street, the Model Prison at Holloway, the admirable improvements and enlargements of the Gaol of Newgate, attest the disinterested application of the funds thus obtained. But how is faith to be kept with their creditors, if their property be snatched from their hands, and with it all means of making repayment? If the Legislature deem it just and expedient to deprive the Corporation of one of their chief sources of revenue, they are bound to release them from all obligations incurred through the possession of those sources. It is not disputed that the Corporation were justified in raising money upon these securities. If, therefore, the securities be arbitrarily confiscated by Parliament, it is to Parliament alone that the holders of those securities must look for redress. But whence are funds to be obtained for future improvements? It would be well if the "faithful Commons" would take the trouble to find a satisfactory answer to this obvious inquiry before they finally decide on ruining the City of London.

PART II.

THE CIVIC REFORM BILL.

The Commission of Inquiry — The New Wards — Aldermen and Common
Councilmen — City Expenditure — City Receipts and Removal of Restrictions.

The Commission of Inquiry.

In the year 1834 a commission was appointed "to inquire into the existing state of the municipal corporations, and to collect information respecting their defects." These commissioners applied themselves to the discharge of their somewhat invidious duties with both earnestness and impartiality, and in their Report, published in 1837, acknowledged the superior excellence of the London Corporation as compared with other corporate bodies. They readily admitted that the Common Council possessed the necessary powers to effect whatever reforms might have become necessary through the lapse of time. They also bore witness that the Corporation had already of itself corrected much that was amiss in its constitution, and that its history furnished "honourable testimonials to the vigilance, good sense, and justice of its legislative body." On these grounds the Imperial Legislature expressly exempted the City of London from the action of the Municipal Corporations Act, and left it in the undisputed enjoyment of its ancient franchises — which, moreover, are declared by 2 William & Mary not to be liable to confiscation. A period of twenty years then passed away without any cause of complaint having occurred to justify the interference of Government, until some disputes arose on the subject of the City markets, and the conservancy of the Thames. Sir George Grey at once availed himself of this pretext to appoint a commission to investigate "the existing state of the Corporation of the City of London, and to collect information respecting its constitution, order, and government." These commissioners, unlike their predecessors, exhibited from the commencement of their proceedings a strong bias and feeling of hostility against the Corporation. The witnesses they called before them were, with scarcely an exception, the avowed enemies of the existing state of things, and prepared to convert trifling blemishes into radical and monstrous defects. And yet even these did not agree among themselves, or assign any sound reasons to render compulsory innovations expedient or justifiable. The general tenor of their evidence, indeed, was actually in favour of the Corporation, when due allowance is made for the spirit by which they were actuated. Nevertheless, it was upon the report of this one-sided and unconstitutional commission that the late ministry founded their Bill for "the better Regulation of the Corporation of the City of London." They had arrived at a foregone conclusion, and asked for only the shadow of an excuse to mask their preconcerted designs against the chief and last stronghold of self-government. The fate of the Corporation was clearly doomed from the hour the House of Commons sanctioned the appointment of a prejudiced and illegal tribunal.

The New Wards.

The first clause of the proposed Bill directs a new division of the City, and recommends that it be redistributed into sixteen wards, instead of twenty-five as heretofore. No reason is assigned for this innovation, beyond an allusion to the fact that no other city—not even Liverpool—possesses more than that number of divisions or departments. The object of the Government was evidently to abase and humiliate the City of London, and to reduce it to the level of the provincial municipalities. It is alleged, that while the metropolis has extended far and wide in every direction, the boundaries of the City have remained unchanged, so that they now inclose barely 1/108th part of the entire metropolitan area. The population also does not embrace 1/20th part of the inhabitants of the aggregate of villages and boroughs collectively known as London. An undue importance, therefore, has been ascribed to that small portion which constitutes the City proper, to the prejudice of the more populous districts, which inclose it on every side. This overrated influence is now to be diminished in good earnest, and henceforth the sole criterion of importance is to be the number of men, women, and children existing within a certain area. Intelligence, wealth, enterprise, industry, commercial reputation, and ancient rights are to be regarded as of little value when compared with the register of births and marriages. So, the City of London is to be divided into sixteen wards, that it may learn not to lift up its head above other corporations. The division is, of course, to be effected by the inevitable barrister of seven years' standing — the modern type of all that is wise, good, intelligent, and incorruptible. It matters not that these gentlemen may and must be totally unacquainted with local peculiarities and requirements. There may be ward charities, and ward bequests, which will create confusion and perplexity under any new arrangement. The inhabitants, too, of one ward may have strong personal objections to be transferred to another. They may dislike the disrupture of old family ties and connections, and cling fondly to the traditions and associations of their youth. Such considerations as these, however, have no weight with red-tapists, who believe in the infallibility of precedents, and apply one measure and one standard to all things.

The only plausible objection that can be urged against the existing distribution of the wards is their inequality as to extent and population; but even if like portions of territory were set apart for each ward, the number of the inhabitants and their influence will vary according to circumstances far beyond the control of any barrister, be he of twice seven years' standing. Besides, though unequal as to area and inmates, the wards are fairly enough represented; for, while the Lime Street Ward returns only four members to the Common Council, Bishopsgate sends fourteen, and Farringdon Without sixteen. This, after all, is surely the point most worthy of attention. The object is not so much to obtain an equality of districts as an equality of representation. It is of no consequence that Cornhill be twice as populous as Bassishaw, if it return twice the number of representatives, for in that case the disparity at once ceases to exist. Sir George Grey, however, is partial to arithmetical equality. There must be sixteen wards and ninety-six Common-Councilmen, or six to each ward. Not that there is anything novel or original in this suggestion. Sir George merely purposes to revert to the arrangements which prevailed in the reign of Richard II. — a period few students of history would select as an illustration of the happiest and most constitutional balance of power throughout all departments of the commonwealth. No proof is adduced that this parcelment of the City was attended with the best possible results, to justify its restoration in the present century, after so long an interval and such elemental changes of the social and commercial system. It is quite possible, and not at all unlikely, that in the time of the second Richard ninety-six Common-Councilmen may have been amply sufficient to discharge all the duties that devolved upon them. But it does not thence follow that that same number will now suffice. If it is proposed by Sir George Grey to establish the civic administration on the broadest, safest, and least assailable foundation, it is scarcely consistent to begin by narrowing that basis. It is generally believed that it is more difficult to corrupt or influence a large number of persons than a small one. In the multitude of counsellors there is strength of will, integrity of purpose, and variety of knowledge. There is less opportunity for jobbing among two hundred than among one hundred individuals, The smaller number is certainly more likely to come to a mutual understanding among themselves, and to apportion to each member his share of the loaves and fishes. On this head no better evidence need be adduced than the report of the commissioners of 1855, by no means too favourably disposed towards the Corporation. It is in the following terms that they speak of the City, and of the advantages incidental to a large representation:-"The antiquity, extent, and importance of its privileges, the long series of its charters, the large amount of its revenues, its metropolitan position, and its historical associations, combine to give it a character different from that of any other municipal borough. It may be added, that the continued predominance of the popular element in the formation of its governing body furnished a reason in 1835 for excepting it from the Municipal Corporations Act; seeing that one of the principal defects which that Act was intended to remedy was the practical exclusion of the principle of popular election from the government of the borough, and the accumulation of power in the hands of a small body of persons. The commissioners state, in their general report of 1835:—'The most common and most striking defect in the constitution of the municipal corporations of England and Wales is, that the corporate bodies exist independently of the communities among which they are found. The corporations look upon themselves, and are considered by the inhabitants, as separate and exclusive bodies; they have powers and privileges within towns and cities from which they are named, but in most places all identity of interest between the corporation and the inhabitants has disappeared.' From the defect described in this passage, the Corporation of London has for many years been exempt. The manner in which the Common Council is elected has produced, to a great extent, an identity of interests between the governing municipal body and the existing municipal community, and has secured to the latter a council representing their general opinions and feelings. The Municipal Commissioners particularly advert to the Common Council of London, as distinguishing that corporation from the close corporations which then prevailed throughout the country."

It is difficult to imagine a better reason for upholding the existing order of things than this very report of the commissioners. They admit that there is an identity of interests between the governing and the governed, between the representatives and their constituents, between the stewards and those for whom they act. No higher commendation can be desired. The system is described as giving satisfaction to all concerned in its operation, and as being free from the great defect which vitiated the municipal arrangements of other cities. The administrative power is not accumulated in the hands of a few, but is freely intrusted to an ample number of representatives chosen by popular election, and liable to removal at the expiration of a year. The fact that the votes of the citizens are usually given to their representatives of many years' standing, is an indisputable proof that the latter do not neglect their duty, or overlook the identity of interests that exists between the governing body and the municipal community. And yet, in the teeth of this report, and in defiance of this good accord, the very defect is to be introduced which was reprobated in other corporations. The administrative power is to be vested in the hands of a comparatively small governing body, and an opportunity afforded for those practices which were considered so objectionable elsewhere.

It is perhaps hardly worthy of remark that the selection of the persons to be appointed to set out the new wards should rest with the Secretary of State. Were it not for the constant augmentation of patronage afforded by each innovation, very little would ever be heard about reform of any kind. But every change, every act of abolition, affords am irresistible opportunity for providing for poor relations and importunate constituents. The Secretary of State, therefore, reserves to himself the choice of the "fit person or persons," which might more decently have been left to the citizens themselves. It is true the latter have not been altogether forgotten, and will not be altogether passed over. To them is to be assigned the privilege of paying five guineas a day to each of these "fit persons," as a recompense for their exertions in introducing confusion and perplexity where order and contentment now prevail.

Aldermen and Common-Councilmen.

The contemplated reduction of the governing body of the City is based upon a specious theory, which will soon be found to be utterly untenable. It is pretended that if the Courts of Aldermen and of Common Council were rendered more exclusive, it would be considered a greater distinction to belong to them, and that consequently a more wealthy and influential class of individuals would seek to be elected. In the first place, the exclusiveness sought to be established in the Corporation of London is the very blot which the Municipal Act was intended to remove from other corporate bodies. What was in them a blemish, is to be engrafted as a beauty into the City of London. But granting that a certain degree of exclusiveness may be not only unobjectionable, but even desirable, is it so very certain that opulent bankers and men of high standing in the commercial world will be thereby induced to offer themselves as candidates for civic offices? Have they themselves offered any suggestion to this effect, or asked for any such motive to do their duty as freeborn citizens? Nothing of the kind. It is pure assumption to assert that when the honour is more difficult of attainment it will become an object of ambition to the mighty men on 'Change. The witnesses who gave evidence on this head before the commissioners were unanimous as to the cause that keeps our princely merchants aloof from the civic arena: it is want of time. One and all declared that they could not spare the time from their own pursuits and engagements. Private interests have more weight with them than those of a public nature; they wish no harm to their fellow-citizens, but will not sacrifice their own comfort or profits to toil for their benefit. Indeed, it is by no means manifest that bankers and merchants are the fittest persons to administer the affairs of the City. As a rule, their homes are as remote as possible from the scene of their daily labours. They know nothing whatever of their neighbours, and care no more for one ward than for another, all being equally indifferent to them. They are bound together by no common ties, nor have they any local or traditional sympathies. It is, therefore, very doubtful that their presence among the aldermen, or in the Court of Common Council, would prove at all beneficial to the City, or likely to enhance their own personal reputation. And if, as they themselves allege, they have hitherto been deterred from undertaking civic duties by the pressure of private affairs, there is no ground for the hypothesis that they will henceforth have more leisure to devote themselves to promoting the welfare of their neighbours. In truth, the office of alderman is no sinecure. He is not merely a very stout gentleman, wearing a blue gown, and guzzling enormous quantities of turtle-soup. That caricature is of a piece with the old fable of the lean Frenchman, starving upon frogs, and capable only of dancing and grimacing. An alderman of the City of London has most onerous duties to discharge, for which he expects no other remuneration than the approval of his own conscience and the respect of his fellow-citizens.

It is matter of public notoriety, that in the year 1834 the Corporation cheerfully complied with the requisitions of the Government with regard to the business of the Central Criminal Court. The number of sessions and of courts was increased, prison accommodation considerably enlarged, and other arrangements made with the utmost liberality in order to facilitate the administration of justice. By the Act passed in that year, it was specially provided that the aldermen of London should be members of the commission, which should be presided over by the Lord Mayor. The local knowledge possessed by these magistrates has enabled them on very many occasions to render important service to the judges in apportioning the punishment due to offenders. At the same time they acquired, on their part, a practical knowledge of the administration of law. The result of this training displayed itself in the soundness of their magisterial decisions, and the correctness of their application of criminal law. Six aldermen are placed on the rota for each month, and compelled to attend at the Old Bailey, unless they can furnish a sufficient excuse for their absence. If the number of aldermen be reduced to sixteen, it is not easy to perceive how this important branch of their duties is to be adequately discharged. In addition to their compulsory attendance at the Central Criminal Court, the aldermen are called upon to exercise various other magisterial functions, including the inspection and management of prisons. They have likewise to attend at the London Quarter Sessions; the special sessions for hearing appeals; the special sessions for licenses; the petty sessions; the special sessions; the Southwark Quarter Sessions, and the annual meetings and adjournments. Even this enumeration of duties, however, is no equivalent indication of the work to be gone through, the whole of which is done gratuitously and without expectation of reward. It is proposed, indeed, that the Court of Mayor and Aldermen of the City of London in the Inner Chamber shall retain the power of appointing the Recorder and certain other officers, and of exercising a supervision over the internal discipline of prisons, and in relation to charities and other trusts, but in most other respects their privileges and jurisdiction are to terminate.

On some points the Common Council are to be exalted at the expense of the Court of Aldermen. They are to administer the money and funds of the City, subject to the audit of three persons annually elected, an abstract of whose statement is to be laid before Parliament. The Corporation are therefore deemed unworthy or incompetent to manage their own finances. Men of business are told that their ignorance is so crass, or their honesty so doubtful, that the Legislature is compelled to keep a watchful eye on their expenditure. The proposition is as absurd as it is insulting and uncalled for. The Corporation are further to have no power to sell, mortgage, or lease their own estates. It may, perchance, be true, that in former times less regard was paid to the discovery of secure and profitable investments than suits the more grasping spirit of the present times. It may also be that greater extravagance was occasionally exhibited than would now be either justifiable or tolerable. But on neither of these grounds was it fitting to affix such a stigma, to pass such a vote of censure, on the existing governing body. Many economical reforms have of late years been spontaneously introduced, and an unmistakable tendency shown to make such further retrenchments as might be consistent with the efficiency of the public service. No doubt the expenses attendant on the collection of the City's income are susceptible of reduction, nor would it be amiss if the heavy outlay connected with the civic government were lightened of some of its items. Still, these are mere questions of detail, and might fairly be left to the good taste, judgment, and discretion of the municipal magistrates. The steps already taken by the Common Council clearly evince their desire to keep pace with the liberalism of the age. Since the year 1835, the sum of at least 100,000 pounds has been offered on the altar of public opinion by the gradual abolition of the fines and fees which restricted the freedom of the City. In the same spirit they sacrificed the street tolls, which annually produced upwards of 5,000 pounds, as soon as they had redeemed the mortgage which enabled them to lay out the new street running north from Farringdon Street. They have also courted publicity, by admitting to their deliberations the reporters of the public press, and by publishing minutes of their proceedings and detailed statements of the receipt and expenditure of public moneys. In these and many similar ways they have manifested their anxiety to act in strict good faith towards their constituents, and to do the utmost in their power to promote the welfare of the City of London. No allegations, indeed, have been made against their scrupulously honourable administration of the funds intrusted to their stewardship. Their integrity has never been impugned by their bitterest enemies — the charges that have been brought forward reflect only upon their judgment. They are accused of lavishing untold sums upon idle pageantry and luxurious entertainments, while they have neglected to improve the great thoroughfares, to cleanse the river, and generally to embellish the metropolis and ameliorate the sanitary condition of its inhabitants. It is worth while to consider how much of truth lies in these accusations.

City Expenditure.

There is no denying that at the first blush it does appear that an unnecessarily large amount of money is laid out annually on festivities. For instance, in the year 1855 upwards of 14,000 pounds were expended on the entertainments given to the Emperor of the French, the King of Sardinia, and the Prefect of the Seine. On minor occasions also very considerable sums are lost in like manner to the City treasury. But this apparent extravagance is not without its advantages. This generous hospitality has rendered the Corporation of London famous throughout the civilized world, and given it a fabulous influence among the nations of the Continent. The chief magistrate of the City is looked upon as only inferior to the sovereign, and far above all other princes and potentates. Thus, in a popular French play the principal personage is made to exclaim in an enthusiasm of ambition — "Yes, I will make myself great; I shall yet be count, marquis, duke, perhaps lord mayor." The credit acquired by the City has been reflected upon the whole nation, and there are none so mean as not to have heard of the wealth, magnificence, and genial hospitality of the free-born citizens of the metropolis of the British empire.

With regard to thoroughfares, it has already been stated that the street tolls were mortgaged for some years, in order to raise the requisite funds for carrying out Farringdon Street to the northern boundary of the City. More recently an enormous debt has been incurred in the construction of Cannon Street. Half a million sterling has been sunk in the attempt to erect a handsome street, which should take off from Cheapside a portion of the exodus to London Bridge, and at the same time furnish a noble example of street architecture. In a pecuniary point of view the experiment has not thus far proved successful, but the very errors of the Corporation are on a grand and magnificent scale. Upwards of another half-million has gone to the construction of the new cattle-market at Islington and the model prison at Holloway. Newgate, also, is being enlarged and improved, and it is proposed to build a lunatic asylum on some lands recently purchased for the purpose in the neighbourhood of Croydon. A very large sum is annually expended in street improvements, besides a contribution of nearly 12,000 pounds a year to a metropolitan fund for objects not comprised within the liberties of the City. The Corporation also pays 11,000 pounds per annum towards the maintenance of the police force, though in other metropolitan districts this proportion of the expenses is debited to the Consolidated Fund. Of the charitable donations and subscriptions of the Corporation it is needless to speak, for their fame has gone forth throughout the world. The City of London School was built at a cost of 20,000 pounds, and year by year receives substantial support and encouragement. The education and maintenance of a hundred orphan children are provided for at another establishment; nor is there any charitable institution worthy of support that is not assisted with ungrudging liberality.

The conservancy of the Thames is another of the responsible duties of the Corporation. For all purposes of navigation the river is admirably adapted by nature, and improved by the thoughtful vigilance of its conservators. As a navigable river the Thames is actually in a better condition at the present day than at any period of its past history, a remark that cannot be applied to any other tidal river in the world. As for the filthy and polluted character of its waters, that at least cannot be laid to the charge of the Corporation. So far back as the year 1842 the City authorities issued a commission to survey and report upon the state of the Thames, and in accordance with the report of those gentlemen proceeded to take measures for embanking the river so as to prevent the deposit of mud on the banks, to deepen the channel, and to improve the wharfage. Strange to say, these spirited proceedings in the interest of the entire metropolis drew down upon the Corporation the wrath of the "Woods and Forests." The foul fermenting accumulations of putrescent matter which send forth the pestilential exhalations that engender so much disease, are declared to be the property of the Crown, as "seised of the ground and soil of the coasts and shores of the sea, and of all the navigable rivers within the flux and reflux of the tide throughout the kingdom." Thanks, therefore, to this precious prerogative of the Crown, her Majesty's lieges have for the last fifteen years continued to be poisoned "by virtue of the common law," while the Corporation have been punished by the infliction of a suit in Chancery for seeking to cleanse the river and purify the atmosphere, without first invoking the wisdom of the "Woods and Forests."

If the crown lawyers be correct, it will follow that the entire seaboard of Great Britain and Ireland is the actual property of the Crown, as well as all lands reclaimed from the sea, and that all other manorial rights are purely imaginary and unfounded.

Hitherto the tonnage rates levied on vessels in the port of London are admitted to have been as moderate as was consistent with the due maintenance of the port. The citizens, being themselves engaged in trade, have always been interested in holding out inducements for the shipping of all nations to frequent their port, and have thus systematically reduced the tonnage dues to the lowest possible scale. The Government, however, looking only to the actual amount of revenue to be obtained, intimate the probability of a future augmentation of these dues. The effect of even a trifling increase will naturally be to divert a portion of the trade to other ports, and to inflict a proportionate amount of injury on the port of London. Such will be the first fruits of Government interference, such the inevitable result of superseding customs and usages which have grown out of the character of the Anglo-Saxon race.

City Receipts.

It has already been stated that in order to carry out street improvements and the construction of public buildings, the Corporation has incurred a very considerable amount of debt. These pecuniary obligations, however, were not rashly undertaken. There was excellent security to offer for their gradual but certain redemption; nor is it anywhere affirmed that the governing body exceeded their powers, or evinced a want of proper caution and foresight. The money raised was applied to just and legitimate purposes, and secured on revenues enjoyed from time immemorial, the usufruct of which might fairly be deemed perpetual. Prescriptive right, however, is no barrier to reformers greedy of patronage, whose only thought is to buy cheap popularity by yielding to vulgar prejudices at the expense of their neighbours. It is thus proposed to abolish all metage dues, to deprive the Corporation of their portion of the coal duties, to remove all restrictions upon brokers, and to sanction the establishment of additional markets within the prescribed distance of seven miles. Nothing is more easy than to pull down and destroy, but to fill up the vacancy thus created is a very different matter. It requires no great amount of moral courage, or of power, to dry up the sources whence the corporate funds are derived, but far less easy will it be to obviate the consequences of a step so ill-judged. It is one thing to demand the usual tale of bricks when the supply of straw is cut off, and another to obtain it. In vain will the Government call upon the City to construct prisons and asylums, to widen the thoroughfares, to cleanse the river, to embellish the streets. Such work as this can only be accomplished through the employment of large funds, and these will no longer be at the disposal of the Corporation. In the first place it is proposed to take away "all such right of metage of any grain, fruit, wares, or merchandise as the Corporation is entitled to by custom, charter, or otherwise." In other words, 11,000 pounds a year of the income of the City is to be confiscated for nobody's benefit, but simply out of deference to a senseless clamour. The officers employed in the collection of this revenue are to receive compensation out of a fund provided for the purpose by a duty of three farthings on every quarter of grain, seed, and pulse brought into the port of London. But nothing is said about compensating the Corporation by remitting their annual contribution to the expenses of the police force, and by defraying the same out of the Consolidated Fund. However, there is cause for gratitude that a still more serious loss is not yet to be inflicted upon the ways and means of the City. The metage duty on coals which may belong to the Corporation after the year 1862, under 1 & 2 William IV., and 8 & 9 Victoria, is not to be affected by the present Bill; but he must be a confiding and unsuspecting individual who can trust to a long enjoyment of that source of income. It is now commonly supposed that the Corporation receive the entire duty of thirteen pence per ton, whereas their actual share of the impost is only fourpence. The remaining nine-pence are taken by the Metropolitan Board of Works, for the general benefit of the capital of the British empire. Against this arrangement no valid objection can be urged, but it is at least unfair to throw the odium of the tax upon those who derive the smallest benefit from its proceeds. It was upon the security of this revenue that the Corporation were enabled to raise the 580,000 pounds required for the construction of Cannon Street. From the same hitherto secure source of income, two millions and a half sterling have been expended on City improvements since the reign of William and Mary. But whence are means to be obtained for carrying out any enterprise of large utility if this revenue be confiscated? It is, besides, not a little characteristic of the late, perhaps of every ministry, that not a word has been said about the surrender of the nine-pence per ton received by the Government. The City alone is to be made the scape-goat—the least offending party is to be sacrificed to screen the real delinquents,—the Corporation is to be thrown overboard, that the ministerial vessel may be the more easily righted. Equally silent was Sir George Grey on the subject of compensation. And yet, when it pleased the Legislature to take from the Duke of Richmond the duty of one shilling per chaldron on coals shipped in the Tyne for home consumption, which had been granted to the family by Charles II., it was deemed only just and equitable to make a reasonable compensation to his grace. The duty at that time (1799) yielded some 21,000 pounds a year, and was commuted for a perpetual annuity of 19,000 pounds, payable out of the Consolidated Fund. In like manner the Duke of Grafton was indemnified in 1806 for loss incurred through the resumption of the "prisage and butlerage" of wines; nor was Lord Gwydir permitted to suffer by the compulsory surrender of his lease in the mooring-chains. In the reign of William IV. the Crown claimed and received a compensation of 300,000 pounds for giving up the passing tolls, and the Corporation itself was awarded upwards of 160,000 pounds on the abolition of the "package and scavage" dues. But if such zeal for retrenchment and economical reform fills the breasts of modern statesmen, how comes it that they have no qualms about retaining the duty of four shillings on every ton of tin extracted from Cornwall, and which swells the revenues of the duchy? In what respect, in short, is the tenure by which the duchy is held more sacred and inviolable than that which entitles the Corporation to the permanent possession of its various sources of income? It were well that the advisers of the Crown first cleared away all obstructions and nuisances front their own precincts, before undertaking to cleanse the premises of their neighbours. But it is far easier to preach than to practise, and to detect the failings of others than to correct one's own.

Another "liberal" clause repeals any charter or grant which prevents the holding any new market within seven miles of the city. The framers of the Bill appear to have overlooked, or laughed to scorn, the ancient common law of the land which prohibits the establishment of any fair or market within "a third part of twenty miles" from one already in existence. This common-law right has been further specially confirmed, so far as the City of London is concerned, by an Act of Parliament in the reign of the third Edward. But considerations of mere law cannot be expected to have much weight with those who have resolved upon setting at naught the eternal principles of justice and equity. Little did the wolf care which way the stream ran, when once he had made up his mind to dine upon lamb.

Yet one other proof of "liberality" before we close these desultory observations. At present the Corporation exercises a watchful surveillance over all persons acting as brokers within the City of London. No one, indeed, is permitted to carry on that highly responsible business without the previous sanction of the Court of Aldermen. This restriction is admitted to have been most beneficial to the public, and the brokers themselves are fully sensible of its advantage to themselves by inspiring a reasonable confidence in their honour and respectability. All this, however, is to be done away with. Government care for none of these things. They prefer punishment to prevention. Let every man do as seemeth good in his own eyes, provided only that he escape conviction for evildoing. In that case the "majesty of the law" will be vindicated by the house of correction or the gallows. Why then take any thought to check the downward step? That is the province of parents, masters, and pastors. The wisdom of the Legislature cannot stoop to such elemental questions. It is unworthy of the wise and illustrious senators of this great empire to take heed of such a vulgar consideration as commercial morality. This is a free country, wherein every man may freely live, providing for himself, and warring upon his kind. Such throughout is the tone and the spirit of the proposed measure for the "better regulation" of the City of London. If this is better, it is devoutly to be hoped that no future ministry will bring forward a Bill for the "best regulation." Every additional step in this direction can only be worse than its predecessor, for the goal to be attained is not only the ruin of civic influence, but the subversion of self-government throughout the realm.

For the present, indeed, this precious Bill has been withdrawn; but let not a suspension of hostilities be construed into a conclusion of peace. The question will certainly be brought before Parliament under a modified form in the ensuing Session, and it is then that the fate of the Corporation will be decided.

Are the citizens of London—are the people of Great Britain—prepared to resign without a struggle the last of the glorious rights and privileges bequeathed to them by their Saxon ancestors? Are they willing to exchange their old ancestral customs and usages for the dogmatic theories and arbitrary practices of continental systems? In short, will they consent to barter freedom for absolutism,

the happiness and independence of the many for the aggrandizement of the few? For that is the real question at issue, and one the
answer to which cannot be much longer deferred.

54